Now You Are Six

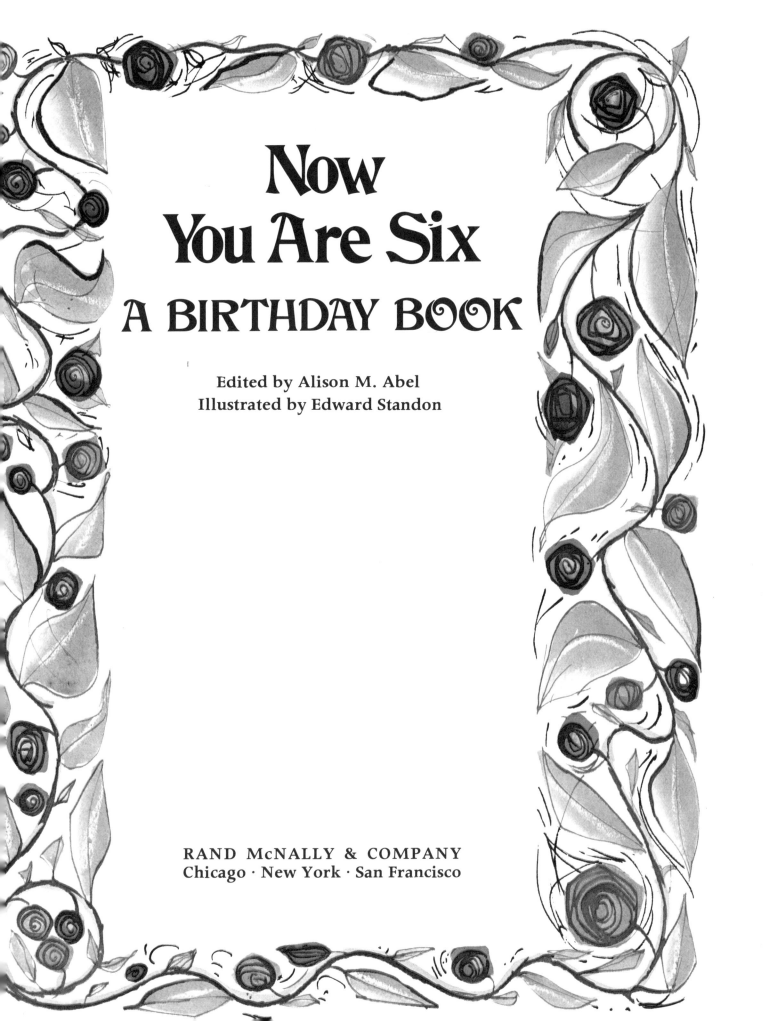

Now You Are Six

A BIRTHDAY BOOK

Edited by Alison M. Abel
Illustrated by Edward Standon

RAND McNALLY & COMPANY
Chicago · New York · San Francisco

Published in the U.S.A.
by Rand McNally & Company 1973
ISBN 0-528-82193-8

© Ward Lock Limited London 1973

First published in Great Britain 1973 by Ward Lock
Limited, 116 Baker Street, London, W1M 2BB

Text filmset in 16pt Apollo
by Keyspools Ltd, Golborne, Lancs

Printed and bound in Belgium
by Casterman S.A., Tournai.

CONTENTS

The Happy Birthday

I wonder if you know what a leprechaun is? Well, he's a sort of Irish elf. The Irish people sometimes call leprechauns the 'Little People'. And little they certainly are. About six inches high at the most—without

their boots on. Usually they wear suits of green velvet, with shiny gold buttons and buckles, and some of them wear little crooked hats on their heads. Leprechauns are very happy creatures as a rule, always singing, dancing, making music—or making mischief!

But there was once a leprechaun who was not very happy, and his name was Mr. Flanagan. He didn't have any first name, for his parents were rather absent-minded and had forgotten to give him one. So he was always known as Mr. Flanagan.

Mr. Flanagan was nearly always sad and gloomy. But every year, on his birthday, he was always sadder and gloomier than ever. Now leprechauns don't have birthday presents like you and me. Instead they have huge, wonderful parties with lots of delicious things to eat and drink. But best of all is the music. At every leprechaun's birthday party there is nonstop singing and dancing and making of music. Fiddles, whistles, pipes and drums all play together, making the most exciting sounds you've ever heard. It is impossible *not* to want to dance to that music.

And that was the reason Mr. Flanagan was so sad. You see, he couldn't sing, he couldn't dance, and he couldn't play any musical instruments at all! He was probably the only unmusical leprechaun in the whole of Ireland. He couldn't even bang a drum in time.

One year, on his birthday, Mr. Flanagan got up very early and went to his own special spot, a lake in the middle of the forest, to be sad all

alone. He was sitting there, thinking miserable thoughts, when suddenly he heard a voice.

'Now what is a young fellow like you doing saddening a lovely day like this?' said the voice.

Mr. Flanagan looked up and there, sitting on a rock next to him, was another leprechaun—one he'd never met before.

'Let me introduce myself,' said the stranger. 'The name is Patrick O'Song, the wanderer. I was just passing through these parts when I heard there was to be a birthday party today. Not being one to miss a good party, I thought I'd stop a while and join in the celebrations. And what do I find—someone looking as miserable as if it's the dentist he's going to and not a party.'

Mr. Flanagan looked as if he was going to cry.

'I wish I was going to the dentist instead of this party,' he said. 'There'll be all that singing and dancing and making of music and everyone having such a grand time and me not being able to sing or dance or play anything at all.'

Patrick O'Song looked shocked. 'Oh, you poor fellow!' he said. 'You can't sing or dance or play? That is the most terrible thing I've ever heard. And you a leprechaun too!'

'Yes,' went on Mr. Flanagan. 'And if that isn't bad enough—the party's to celebrate *my* birthday!' And he began to cry, his big tears making ripples on the still water of the lake.

'Oh, come now, my friend,' Patrick pleaded. 'Don't be making too much water or you'll be overflowing the lake and flooding the whole forest. Don't forget the old saying: "There's never a rainy day so dark that the yellow sun won't dare to shine on it".'

Mr. Flanagan had to admit that he had never heard that saying before.

'No? Well, I must admit I just made it up,' Patrick grinned. 'But it's true nonetheless. It just so happens that I can help you and help you I will. I am going to give you a birthday present.'

'What's a birthday present?' asked Mr. Flanagan. (Remember, leprechauns don't have birthday presents like we do.)

'Oh, it's a custom that human people have,' explained Patrick. 'They give each other little presents on their birthdays—chocolates and pairs of socks and handkerchiefs and such like. It's an odd custom, but fun just the same. Now, as I told you, my name is Patrick O'Song, and I'm called that for a very special reason. I have magic powers to give others the gift of song. And that's what I'll give you. Then not only will you be able to sing, but you'll sing *all the time!* You'll become the most famous singing leprechaun in the land.'

Mr. Flanagan could hardly believe his ears. He was going to be able to sing. His tears stopped and a smile spread across his face.

'Me—sing?' he cried. 'Really? How wonderful!'

'Now,' Patrick went on, 'look at me and look at me hard. When I'm gone and you can see me no more, the magic will have worked. You will no longer be known as Mr. Flanagan the gloomy one. You'll be be Flanagan the famous singing leprechaun.'

Patrick's eyes twinkled mischievously.

Mr. Flanagan stared at Patrick who slowly began to fade away until there was nothing to be seen of him but the two twinkling lights that were his eyes. Then, slowly, they too faded.

Mr. Flanagan couldn't wait to find out if the magic had worked. He opened his mouth and sang:

'I can sing, I can sing,
I can make the valleys ring,
With my voice singing clear,
I can sing without fear.'

The magic had worked—he could sing! He didn't know where the words came from. They just came out as he sang.

Mr. Flanagan ran home to tell his friends what had happened. It wasn't long before he came across two of them practicing a dance for the party.

'Hello, Mr. Flanagan,' said one of them,

whose name was Dingle O'Dell. 'You're looking happy for once. Are you looking forward to your birthday party?'

Mr. Flanagan opened his mouth, meaning simply to say 'Hello' to his friends. But instead he found himself singing:

'Mr. Flanagan would like to say,
Hello to you this fine old day!'

Dingle nearly fell over in astonishment. 'Mr. Flanagan!' he cried. 'Was that you singing?'

'Yes, I can sing,
I can sing,
I can sing,
Like anything'

Mr. Flanagan's friends were so surprised they both fell over backward. Then they scrambled to their feet and ran off to the leprechaun's village as fast as their legs would take them, shouting at the tops of their voices: 'Mr. Flanagan can sing! Mr. Flanagan can sing!'

It was true. Mr. Flanagan could sing. In fact it appeared he couldn't *not* sing. Every time he opened his mouth and tried to speak, what came out was singing—and always in rhyme. Well, Patrick O'Song had said he'd give him the gift of song and make him the most famous singing leprechaun in the land—and it looked as if that was what had happened.

Mr. Flanagan's party was a great success, and nobody enjoyed it quite as much as Mr. Flanagan himself. He sang and danced all night long, until his voice was hoarse and his legs too tired to carry him.

Soon his fame spread throughout all Ireland, and people came from far and wide to visit him and listen to his singing—but Mr. Flanagan didn't mind. He loved singing and he never got tired of it. In fact, he's probably still singing to this day, for leprechauns live for hundreds of years.

And so, as Mr. Flanagan would say:

'The time has come,
to say, my friend,
of this story,
Here's the end!'

MR. NOBODY

I know a funny little man,
    As quiet as a mouse.
He does the mischief that is done
    In everybody's house.
Though no one ever sees his face,
    Yet one and all agree
That every plate we break, was cracked
    by Mr. Nobody.

'Tis he who always tears our books,
    Who leaves the door ajar.
He picks the buttons from our shirts,
    And scatters pins afar.
That squeaking door will always squeak—
    For prithee, don't you see?
We leave the oiling to be done
    by Mr. Nobody.

He puts damp wood upon the fire,
    That kettles will not boil;
His are the feet that bring in mud
    And all the carpets soil.
The papers that so oft are lost—
    Who had them last but he?
There's no one tosses them about
    But Mr. Nobody.

The fingermarks upon the door
    By none of us were made.
We never leave the blinds unclosed
    To let the curtains fade.
The ink we never spill! The boots
    That lying round you see,
Are not our boots—they all belong
    To Mr. Nobody.

FOLLOW THE NOTE

One little note was left behind when someone blew this French horn. Which way must it go to join the other notes coming out of the horn?

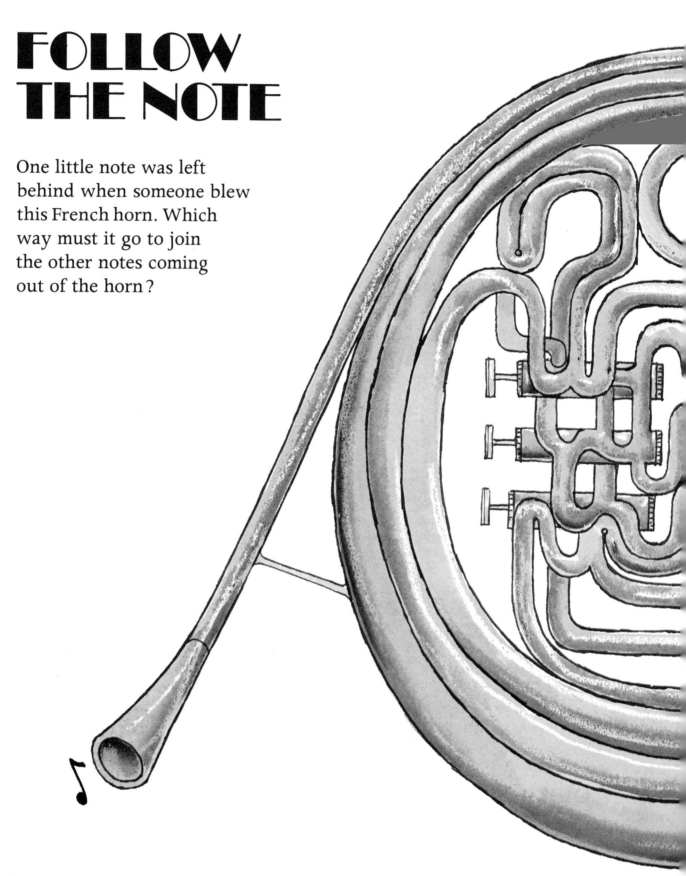

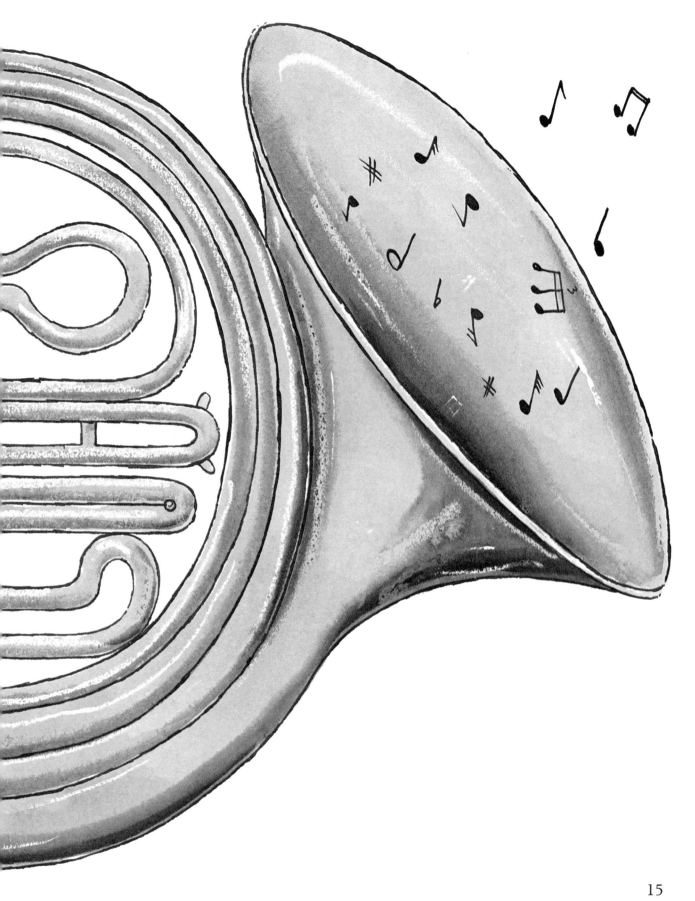

The Dreadful Dragon

Many years ago, there lived a great King who ruled over a beautiful kingdom and many people. Everything in the land was going on very nicely until a dragon, both fierce and big, came and made his home in the mountains not far from the city where the King's palace was. When the dragon went out hunting for his dinner in the forest, he would burn down trees, and generally make a nasty mess of the countryside.

The King, as you can imagine, became very angry at this. He ordered his best soldiers out and told them to kill the dragon. One bright morning his soldiers marched smartly out of the city gates. But none of them returned.

They marched up to the mouth of the cave where the dragon lived. When the dragon saw all the soldiers he was very frightened. This made him breathe out hot flames, and the soldiers were burned to cinders where they stood.

The King was very upset. Then all the people of the kingdom told him that he, and he alone, must get rid of the dragon, because they were much too frightened to do anything themselves.

'What can and what shall I do? cried the King.

'Do what Kings in all the best fairy stories do,' shouted the people. 'Offer your daughter in marriage, together with half of your kingdom, to the young man who rids you of this fierce dragon.'

'What a good idea,' said the King. 'I'll do just that.'

So he sent out heralds to all the outlying districts of his kingdom, with big posters which read:

THE YOUNG MAN WHO RIDS MY KINGDOM OF THE DREADFUL DRAGON SHALL MARRY MY DAUGHTER AND HAVE HALF OF MY BEAUTIFUL KINGDOM
For further details:
Please call at the palace.

Of course princes, nobles and young men of all sorts and sizes came from far and wide, for the sweetness and beauty of the Princess was well-known—and the offer of half a kingdom was a great attraction too!

After a year the dragon was still going strong and there were a good many fewer princes, nobles and young men left in the world.

The King was by now dreadfully worried. Then, one day, at about tea-time, a young man strolled into

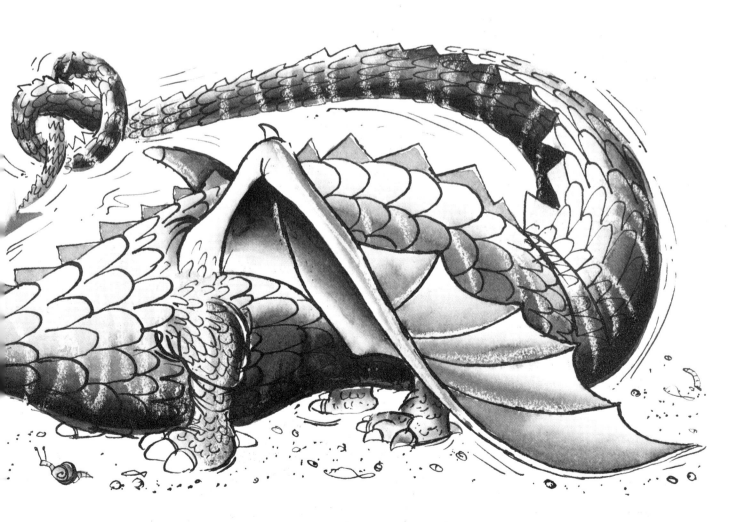

the city and asked the way to the palace. He had round blue eyes and straw colored hair and a mischievous cheerful smile.

When he got to the palace he asked to see the King.

'Go away,' whispered the courtiers. 'The King is too worried to see anyone!'

'No, I won't go away. I've come too far, and anyway I think I can rid him of the dragon,' said the young man.

This made the courtiers sit up and take notice, so at last the young man saw the King.

'May I have your permission, your Majesty, to rid you of your dreadful dragon?' said the young man, bowing low.

'Certainly, you can try', said the King. 'But I don't hold out much hope for you. Do you want to to borrow a suit of armor?'

'No thank you,' said the young man (who, by the way, was called Michael). 'But could you lend me a

gold piece, just until tomorrow evening?'

'Certainly,' said the King, taking one out of his pocket and thinking, 'I don't expect I'll see that gold piece again, but it's cheaper than a suit of armor!'

So Michael bowed low, and with the gold piece jingling in his pocket, left the King and his palace and walked through the city until he came to a shop that sold large looking-glasses. Here he bought the biggest he could carry. Then he bought a bottle of champagne.

After he had eaten lunch, he set off for the dragon's cave, carrying the looking-glass and the bottle of champagne. He arrived at the cave without mishap about two hours before daybreak—just nice time to get everything ready.

First he rolled a huge boulder into place opposite the entrance to the cave. Then he leaned the looking-glass in front of the boulder. This done, he hid behind the boulder and popped the cork of the champagne bottle. The champagne cork whizzed out of the neck of the bottle and into the cave, hitting the dragon on the nose.

The dragon woke up at once and padded to the door of the cave. But the sight of his reflection in the mirror frightened him so much that he turned tail and ran back inside.

Then Michael called out, 'Hey, dragon—come out and fight!'

But the dragon, who had never seen himself or any other dragon before, was too frightened to come out, and he hid his eyes, crying, 'Please go away.'

'Well,' said Michael, 'I'm not moving from here, so if you don't like what you see, I advise *you* to go away—and go away quickly. All you have to do if you really don't want to see that dreadful creature again is to keep on running. Don't look behind you because you don't know what you might see, and I wouldn't like you to be frightened.'

So off went the dragon at great speed, with never a look over his

shoulder. And as far as I know he's still running and running and running, and whenever and wherever he stops he'll never, never look behind him, I can tell you for sure.

As for Michael, he returned to the King and was hailed as a great hero. The King gave him half his kingdom, as he had promised, and the hand of the beautiful Princess in marriage.

GAMES TO PLAY AT YOUR PARTY

NOAH'S ARK

Two children are chosen as Mr. and Mrs. Noah. They stand at one end of the room guarding the entrance to the Ark. The rest of the children pair off and stand in two lines. One line is the decider animals and the other the guesser animals. Each decider chooses what animal he would like to be—but he doesn't tell his partner.

Taking turns, the pairs go up to the Ark with the decider pretending to be an animal. The guesser animal must copy him as closely as he can. When they reach the Ark, Mr. and Mrs. Noah say: "Who comes for a home in the Ark?"

The guesser animal has to say what animal his partner is pretend-

ing to be. If he is right, they go into the Ark. If he guesses wrong, he and his partner are drowned in the flood!

HUNT THE SLIPPER

One player is chosen as the customer. The others, the cobblers, sit cross-legged on the floor in a circle. They pretend to be working very hard mending shoes. The customer comes up to the cobblers carrying a slipper and says: 'Cobbler, cobbler, mend my shoe. Have it done by half-past two.'

The customer gives the shoe to one of the cobblers. Then the cobblers pass the slipper round the ring, under their knees, while the

22

customer runs round trying to get slipper. The cobbler he takes it from is the next customer.

HOW MANY TEETH, MR. BEAR?
One of the children is chosen as Mr. Bear. He sits in the middle of a circle. The others creep forward, asking: 'How many teeth, Mr. Bear?'

If Mr. Bear growls 'One' or 'Two' —or any number except 'Twenty'— they are quite safe and can still creep forward. But when Mr. Bear says 'Twenty—very sharp', he leaps to his feet and chases the children.

All those he has touched before they are back holding hands in the circle drop out of the game. The last one left is the next Mr. Bear.

THE DONKEY'S TAIL
Before the party, draw a donkey on a big piece of paper. Draw a tail and cut this out. When you want to play the game, pin the drawing to the wall. The players are then blindfolded in turn, led up to the donkey, and asked to pin the tail on the donkey. The one who pins the tail nearest to the right place is the winner.

The Three Wishes

There was once an old man who lived with his wife in a little tumbledown cottage. The man had worked hard all his life, but still they were very poor. Their children had grown up and left home, so they only had each other for company.

One winter's evening the old couple were sitting by the fire, talking of this and that.

'If only we could have a nice house like our neighbors, instead of this tumbledown cottage,' said the wife.

'And a bigger stable,' added the old man, 'with a good mule standing in it.'

'And a horse and cart,' went on the wife. 'Then we could go and visit our children.'

As she spoke there was a flash of light, and there before them stood a strange, beautiful figure. It was Mrs. Luck, the good fairy.

The old couple stared at her.

'I heard what you were saying,' said Mrs. Luck. 'You have worked hard all your lives, and now I will grant you three wishes. One for you,' she said to the wife. 'One for you,' she said to the husband, 'and the third wish for both of you. You must wish for something you both want. I shall come back tomorrow and see how your wishes have changed your lives.' And with these words she was gone again.

The old couple could hardly believe that Mrs. Luck had visited them at last. The wife spoke first: 'I would like . . .' she said.

But her husband put his hand over her mouth.

'Wait, my dear,' he said. 'We must think very carefully before we decide what we want. Let's go to bed now. We shall know what to wish for in the morning.'

So off they went to bed. But neither of them could sleep. They tossed and turned, trying to decide the three things they wanted most in all the world.

At last the wife fell into a doze. But she began talking in her sleep. Her husband was afraid that she would wish for something silly in her dreams, so he woke her up again. Then he fell asleep. But he, too, began to talk in his sleep, and the wife woke him up.

So it went on, all night long. By the morning they were both so tired and bad-tempered that they were in no mood to agree about anything.

Grumbling and yawning, they came downstairs for breakfast.

'Well, I've made up my mind,' declared the wife. 'I wish . . .'

At that moment the most delicious smell came drifting across from their neighbor's house.

'Oh, what a lovely smell!' cried the old man. 'Our neighbors must be making sausages again.'

'Yes,' agreed the wife. 'How I wish I could have one for breakfast.'

She had hardly finished speaking when a big, beautiful sausage appeared on her plate. The wife stared at it. She couldn't think how it had got there.

But her husband knew.

'Good gracious!' he shouted. 'Now look what you've done. That's one wish gone. Do you think of nothing but eating and drinking? Oh, I wish that sausage were stuck on the end of your nose!'

At once the sausage flew up from the table and stuck to the end of the old woman's nose. The man was horrified. He, too, had spoken without thinking.

'Look what *you've* done!' cried the wife, running to look at herself in the mirror. She pulled and tugged and twisted at the sausage, but it was firmly stuck to the end of her nose.

'It was your fault,' said the old man. 'If you hadn't made such a silly wish to begin with it would never have happened.'

'If I waste my wish that's my loss, not yours,' retorted the wife. 'But you have wasted our third wish as well, the wish we must both agree on.'

'Why the third?' asked the husband.

'Because we must wish this sausage away, of course,' cried the wife.

'But my dear wife,' said the husband, 'if we do that we won't be able to have a nice new house.'

'That's too bad,' cried the wife.

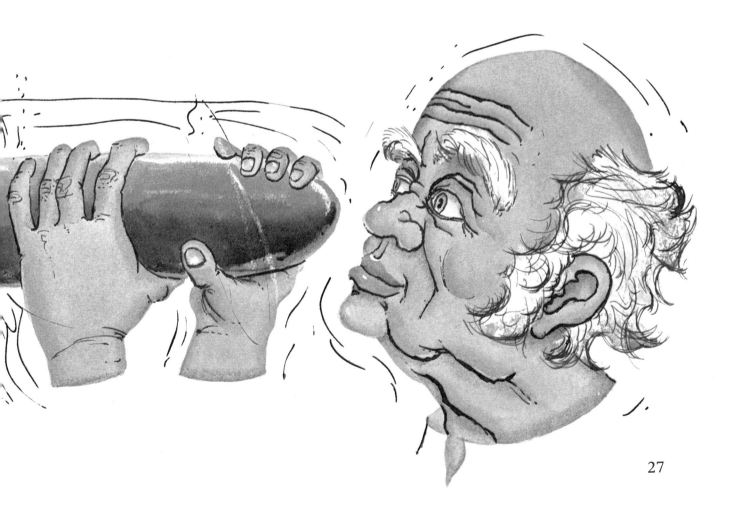

'Or the big stable, with the mule inside it,' went on the husband.

'Who cares?' shrieked the wife.

'Or the horse and cart,' said the old man.

'Then we will have to do without!' screamed the wife, running round and round the room, tugging at the sausage.

'Don't you think you could get used to it?' pleaded the husband. 'Just think, we could wish for a whole mine full of jewels. We'd be so rich you could have a beautiful gold case for your sausage. You might even set a fashion, and all the great

ladies would want one too. They would come from far and wide to see you with a sausage on your nose.'

'No,' sobbed the wife. 'All I want is to be able to see the end of my nose again!'

At last the husband saw there was nothing to be done.

'I wish that sausage was off my wife's nose,' he said, sadly.

No sooner had he said the words than the sausage flew off the old woman's nose and landed on her plate.

'I don't think I could eat that sausage now,' said the old woman.

'In fact, I don't think I could eat a sausage ever again.'

Her husband agreed with her, so they threw it into the street where the neighbors' dog snapped it up and ran away with it.

That evening, as the old couple were sitting by the fire, Mrs. Luck appeared again.

'Well,' she said, 'how have your

three wishes changed your lives?'

'Not at all,' cried the wife. 'And it was all his fault.'

'Nonsense,' retorted the old man. 'She started it.'

And the two began to quarrel again.

'Listen to me,' said Mrs. Luck. 'If you go on quarreling your lives will certainly have changed. You will be more unhappy than ever. But if you learn to be grateful for what you have, and live peacefully together, then you will have gained a great deal.'

With these words the good fairy disappeared. She never visited the old couple again, but they always remembered what she said. And if they ever started to grumble or quarrel, one of them had only to say one word, 'sausage', and they were at peace again.

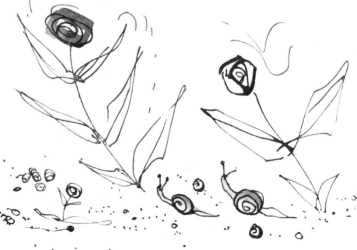

MAKING FINGER PUPPETS

These 'finger puppets' are very easy to make. You can decorate your puppet to look like a pixie, an old fashioned Father Christmas, an angel—or you could make a puppet for each finger and have a whole family.

You will need a piece of stiff paper or thin card, some paints or felt-tip pens, glue, and scraps of thread and cotton wool for decorating.

Draw a circle round a saucer on to a piece of stiff paper or card. Cut out the circle, fold it into quarters, and cut along the fold lines. Each quarter makes one puppet. Bend the quarter into a cone and glue the edges together.

To make the face, cut out a small circle of white paper, draw on the eyes, nose, and mouth, and glue the 'face' to the cone.

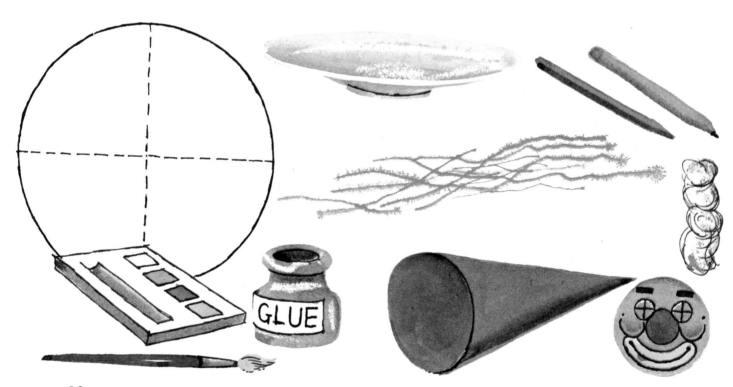

To make the arms, cut out a curved strip of paper like this. Put a little glue in the middle of the strip and stick it to the back of the cone.

You can paint clothes on the body of your puppet and stick on 'hair', using short pieces of wool. To make a hat for your puppet, cut out a small circle of card, make a hole in the middle, and push the point of the cone through the hole.

To make a Father Christmas like your grandparents remember, paint your card red. Cut paper for the arms like this, to make 'sleeves' for his cloak. Make hair and a beard from cotton, and trim the edges of the cloak with cotton or 'lace' cut from a paper doily.

A pixie can be made from green card. Bend the point of the cone a little so that his 'hat' sits at an angle. To make an angel, use white or silver card. Cut out the wings from a piece of card shaped like this and attach them to the puppet with glue. You can add 'glitter' for a sparkling effect.

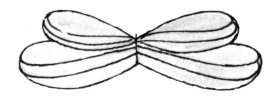

31

The Stray Cat

'I'm sorry children, but you can't keep him,' said Mrs. Black.

'But he likes us,' said Dan.

'And he hasn't got any other home,' said Sarah.

She held the black cat in her arms and rubbed his chin. He purred and stretched out one long black paw in rapture.

'He'll soon find another home,' said Mrs. Black, 'or go back where he came from. Put him outside and don't encourage him to stay. He's had a good meal. Now I must find a a label for this cupboard. Your Aunt Kate wants it for her new house in town.'

Their mother went to find the label, while Dan and Sarah put the cat out in the garden. They felt very sad. The cat was a stray, and they had been feeding him with milk and scraps outside the back door. But now their mother had refused to let them keep him, and they must make him go away.

The young cat sat on the lawn and washed himself—first one ear and then the other. After that he began to chase his tail, spinning over and over like a hoop on the grass.

'Isn't he silly!' said Sarah, and she and Dan both laughed, until they remembered that they couldn't keep the cat. They went into

the shed where they often played, but they didn't feel like playing today. They just talked about the cat, wishing and wishing that they could keep him.

In the road a van drew up. Through the shed window Dan and Sarah saw two men go up the path to the house. The men carried out the cupboard, put it in the van, and drove off.

'Tea's ready!' called Mrs. Black, and Dan and Sarah went indoors.

'Doughnuts!' said Dan. He was sad about the cat—but he was hungry, too!

The cat didn't come back next day, nor the day after that.

'He was such a nice cat,' said Sarah. 'I wish he had stayed.'

'I expect he found a family that wanted him,' said her mother.

'Well, *we* wanted him,' said Dan.

'Cats cost quite a lot of money to feed,' said Mrs. Black.

'But they are useful—they eat mice and rats,' said Dan.

'And birds,' said his mother. 'I like birds.'

'We could have trained him not to kill birds,' said Dan hopefully.

'No,' said his mother. 'You can't train a cat not to follow its instincts, and most cats kill birds. Now, would you like me to read to you? After that I want you to go to bed early. Tomorrow we're going up to town to help Aunt Kate move into her new house.'

'Daddy too?' asked Sarah.

'No, Daddy is going to do some gardening.'

Next morning they set off early in the car and got to Aunt Kate's house just as the moving men had finished unloading the last of her furniture. Aunt Kate, with her hair tied up in a scarf, was staring at the cupboard that had arrived two days earlier.

'Hello,' she called, as Sarah and Dan and their mother trooped in. 'I'm so glad you've come early. There's a very funny noise coming from this cupboard!'

They all listened and heard a faint scratching noise. Sarah took her mother's hand, not sure if she liked it. It sounded as if there were something alive in the cupboard.

'Do you think it's a mouse?' asked Aunt Kate, shuddering. She didn't like mice.

'*I'll* open the door,' said Dan, and he turned the catch and opened the door a little way.

They waited, holding their breath. And then out of the cupboard came a black head and a black body and a long black tail.

'It's our cat!' cried Dan and Sarah.

'Well I never!' said their mother. 'Poor thing, he must have slipped into the cupboard when I wasn't looking. But he's been in there for

nearly three days! How thin he is!'

The cat rubbed himself round Sarah's legs, and rubbed himself round Dan's legs. Then he looked up and mewed.

'He must be starving,' said Aunt Kate. 'Quick, Dan, fetch that bottle of milk from outside the front door. Sarah, find a saucer in that picnic basket.'

Dan poured some of the milk into the saucer, and Sarah put it on the floor. The cat lapped it quickly, then looked for more.

'We'd better not give him any more yet,' said Aunt Kate. 'I wish I had a can of cat food. I didn't expect a cat as a visitor!'

'I brought some cold chicken for our dinner,' said Mrs. Black. 'We'll

give him a little of that—not too much as he hasn't been fed for so long.'

When the cat had eaten the food, he washed himself, then walked about the apartment, sniffing and exploring.

The postman came with a package for Aunt Kate. The cat saw the open door and ran toward it.

'Don't let him get out!' called Mrs.

Black. 'We don't want to lose him now.'

'Do you mean . . .?' began Dan.

His mother laughed. 'Yes. We'll take Puss home with us and keep him. I think he deserves it after all he has been through.'

Sarah rushed to her mother and hugged her, and Dan turned a somersault to show how pleased he was.

'Will he like going in the car?' asked Sarah.

'No,' said her mother. 'Poor Puss has had enough of traveling. Look, Dan, there's that nice big cardboard box there. We'll take him in that. Can you make some holes in the top with your penknife to give him air? Let's hurry and help Auntie, and then we'll soon have Puss safely home.'

When they had helped with the unpacking and were having their picnic dinner, Puss jumped on Sarah's lap, dug with his claws for a moment, then curled up, gave a big sigh, and went fast asleep.

'He knows he's *our* cat now,' said Sarah.

WHAT IS THE TIME?

Before people knew how to make clocks like the ones we have today, they had to find other ways of telling the time.

The ancient Egyptians used a stick planted in the ground. When the sun shone, they could tell what time it was by the direction the shadow of the stick was pointing.

The hours on a sundial were marked on the base, and the shadow from the pointer moved round to show the time.

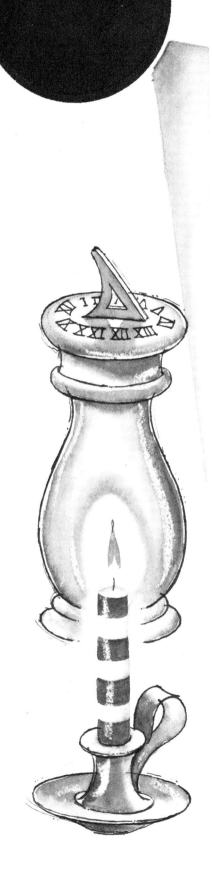

An early water clock was just a can of water with a hole in the bottom. The hours were marked down the inside of the can.

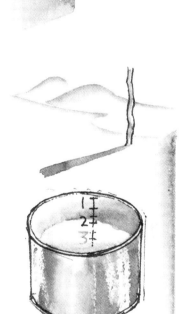

Hourglasses were made of glass and shaped like a figure 8. The sand inside trickled through from the top half to the bottom half.

The hours were marked down the side of a candle clock. People could tell what time it was by noting how far down the candle had burned.

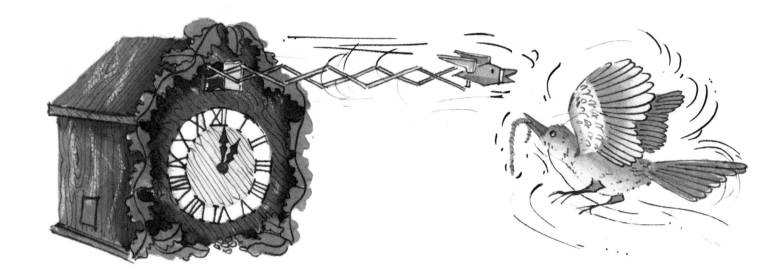

How do you know when it is dinner-time? Do you look at the clock? Or do you know it is time to eat because you feel hungry? When you can tell the time you don't have to ask 'Is it dinner-time yet?' You can look at the clock and that will give you the answer.

A good way to learn to tell the time is to practice with a model clock like the one on the opposite page. You can make this clock quite easily. Trace the triangle and the dotted lines with a pencil. Turn over the tracing paper and put it on a piece of card. If you scribble over the lines you have drawn, they will appear on the card. Cut out the card triangle. Paint or draw the numbers on to the 'face' of the clock. Now make small holes in each corner of the triangle, and one in the middle. Fold the card along the dotted lines. Tie the corners together through the holes with string or ribbon. Cut out the hands in card and make a hole in each one near the straight end. Fix the hands to the clock through the holes with a paper fastener.

You can ask a grown-up to help you work out what time your clock is saying as you turn the fingers.

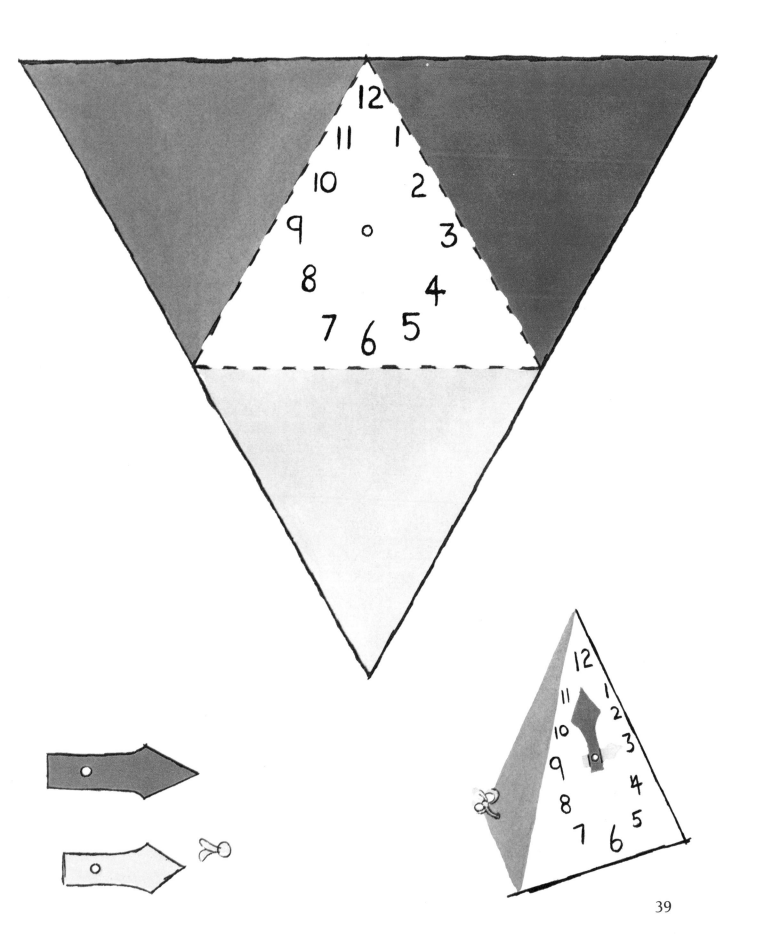

Lions on the Loose

There are eight of us all together. We are all exactly alike, but I was the last one to be made. That's why the others say I'm the youngest. At the time this story begins we each sat proudly on a flat round stone called a 'plinth'. Our manes were magnificent. Our eyes were fierce. Our tails coiled neatly by our feet. We were lions, stone lions. And we all sat in the truck bumping along toward the new school and library.

'I'm going to guard the gates,' said the first lion.

'So am I,' said the second.

'I'm going to stand on one of the lawns,' said the third.

How they boasted! None of them took much notice of me because I'm the youngest.

For several days we just sat in a builder's yard along with bricks and stones and bags of cement. It was very dull. Then one day the head builder, called the foreman, came along. He told his workmen to load us on to a truck. We were going somewhere at last. In fact we were taken to the library. I was disappointed. I had hoped it might be the school. That sounded much more fun.

Outside the grand entrance to the library was a row of stone pillars holding up a low stone wall. Every few yards there was a gap in the pillars. There were eight gaps. Yes, you've guessed right. The gaps had been left for us. Our job was to help hold up the stone wall on our heads. There was a lot of grumbling that night when the workmen went home.

'The indignity of it!'

'My ears are getting squashed.'

'I can't even swish my tail.'

As usual I didn't say very much, but I thought hard. That wasn't very easy, though, with a stone wall on my head.

After three days and nights I decided that I could stand it no longer. I must have a rest from the wall. On the fourth night, as soon as there was a moon, I slipped away. I was very stiff after all that sitting, but my legs soon got moving.

What a wonderful time I had! First I sniffed round the new buildings. There was one nasty moment there. I was so pleased to be out that I wasn't watching where I was going. Suddenly I looked down, and there at my feet was another lion staring up at me—or so I thought. I bent down to have a closer sniff, and ooh, my nose was all wet. Of course, it wasn't another lion at all. It was me reflected in some water. I had nearly walked into a pond!

Later that night I reached the open countryside. I leaped through fields and woods, past farms and villages. I ran as I had never run before, with the moon shining down on me. When it began to get light I decided to go back to the library. As I wearily crept up the steps to the wall, I wondered if the other lions had missed me.

They were awake. I could hear their deep stone voices.

'Fancy just going off like that and leaving us to hold up the wall!'

'Poor Seven's had an awful time down that end!'

Suddenly they saw me. Seven pairs of stony eyes looked angrily at me.

'Where have you been?' said seven gruff voices.

'I . . . well . . . I just went out.'

They all told me what they thought of me, and I got back on my stone feeling very unhappy.

'I'm really sorry,' I said to Seven.

'Don't do it again, please,' said Seven.

My heart sank—never to go out over those fields again, never to run and jump. I

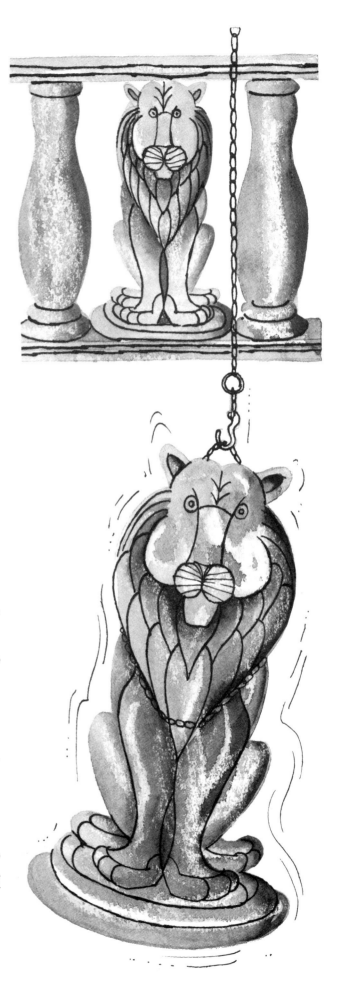

couldn't sit for ever with a stone wall on my head!

'Don't do it again,' repeated Seven. Then he went on, 'That is, unless you can find something else to help hold up the wall.'

That was an idea! All day I thought hard. Then I remembered something I had seen the night before in the builder's yard. That night I whispered to Seven, 'Look, I'm just going to find something else to hold up the wall. Can you manage until I get back?'

In the builder's yard I found what I was looking for. In one corner was a pile of small stone pillars, a little shorter and wider than the ones that held up our wall in between the lions. Perhaps they were left in the corner because they were the wrong size.

I nosed the nearest pillar off the pile, rolled it out of the yard and up the path, round the lake, and bump, bump, bump, up the three steps and over to the wall. The hardest part was getting the pillar upright on my flat stone, but I managed it.

'Gadding off again?' said Number One sternly.

'It's all right,' said Seven. 'He's found a pillar instead.'

'Let me see,' said One, and he edged his way off his stone and creaked and grated his way toward

'Well I never. You are a clever lad. Where did you find those pillars?'

I told them about the builder's yard. That started it. They all wanted one. Soon the place seemed full of lions pushing and pulling at the pillars. When they had finished we all sat back and admired the wall.

'It looks so good,' said Five. 'Need we go back at all?'

'Where could we go?' said One.

'Come with me,' I said. 'I'll show you.'

I led them round the library and over to the school where I had seen a children's playground the night before. I showed them all where I meant them to sit. Number One said we could go off on our own for a while, but we must be back by first light.

There was a terrible fuss in the morning. First the foreman found we were missing from the wall. They soon found us, of course.

'Well, strike me pink,' said the foreman. 'How did they get in the playground?'

'They look very good sitting round the playground. The children will like them,' said one of the youngest builders.

'We must ask the manager,' said the foreman to the builders, and off they went.

The manager came and looked at us. 'We must ask the Authorities,' he said, and off they all went again.

Soon they were back, the builders, the foreman, the manager, and the

43

Authorities. They stood and looked at us.

'We must ask the Mayor,' said the Authorities, and off they went once more.

A little later the builders, the foreman, the manager, and the Authorities returned with the Mayor. They looked at us. They looked at the wall, and then they looked at us again.

'Um,' said the mayor, stroking his beard and frowning.

It was an anxious moment for us. If we had to go back and hold up the wall by the library, it would always be difficult to get away, even at night. When the builders left, what could we use to prop up the wall?

They would be sure to take the spare pillars with them. But if we were allowed to stay in the playground, we would have the children romping round us in the daytime, and at night we would be free to go wherever we liked—no worry about walls.

'Um,' said the Mayor again. 'I think they had better stay in the playground. We can't waste time moving them back. After all, we can't be sure they'd stay in the wall, can we?'

So that's how it all happened. That's how it is that the new school is the only one in these parts that has eight stone lions sitting in the playground.

44

Rory's Holiday

Rory was eating his breakfast in Granny's kitchen in Scotland. Daddy had said, 'When you are six, Rory, you can stay with Granny for the summer holidays.' Now he was a long way, a night and a day in the train, from his home in the city.

'Eat up your porridge, my bonny bairn,' said Granny. Rory liked being called a bonny bairn. That meant Granny thought he was a handsome child—and he was. He had dark red hair and freckles and his cheeks were rosy from the fresh mountain air.

'I'm going out in the boat with Callum today,' Rory told Granny. Callum was his friend. He was a big boy. He was older than Rory.

'Mind you don't fall into the loch!' said Granny.

'I'll be careful,' Rory promised. 'There's a monster in the loch.'

Granny laughed. 'I never heard tell of a monster.'

'Callum has seen it,' Rory insisted. 'It has a little head and a long neck and two humps.'

'Och, away with you!' Granny gave him a little pat. 'Here's Callum. I hear him whistling.'

Rory ran to the door. He was wearing his kilt. He hardly ever wore it at home in London.

'Goodbye, Granny!' Rory called as he and Callum ran off together down the hillside, leaping and shouting. When they had to cross a stream Callum took Rory's hand because the water came rushing down so fast over the stones. On their way they saw a ram with its curly horns caught in a thorn bush.

'Poor beastie!' said Callum, and Rory helped him to set it free. High above them in the sky they could hear a bird calling, 'Pee-weet! Pee-weet!'

'It's a peewit,' said Callum.

Rory looked up, trying to see the peewit.

'I wish we had peewits at home,' he said.

They were nearly at the loch now —only one more wall to scramble over. The water in the loch was dark. Callum said it was very deep.

'A monster could easily be hiding down there,' Rory thought.

'I'll help you to push the boat out, Callum,' he said.

Callum took the oars. He was very strong and rowed well. The sun was shining on the water. It made a golden path across to the island in the middle of the loch. Rory looked back at the shore. He could see some sheep and black cattle grazing, but that was all. There was not another person in sight.

'We'll go to the island,' said Callum.

There was a little stony beach on the island, and Callum showed Rory how to choose a flat stone and how to throw it so that it would skip across the water.

Granny had given Rory some lunch to share with Callum. They sat down in the sun and ate the flat round cakes made of oatmeal called 'bannocks'. Rory had watched Granny baking them on a griddle, which was a big round iron plate with a bow-shaped handle. Granny had given Rory some rowan jelly too.

When they had finished their picnic Callum showed Rory the rest of the island. It was only a small island, but it was fun to explore. There was even a little cave.

'Once a Scottish soldier hid in this cave,' said Callum. 'He was running away from the English. He swam across the loch at night, when it was dark, and the English soldiers never found him.'

'Is he still there?' asked Rory, peering into the cave.

'Och, no! It was a long time ago— more than two hundred years ago when the Scots were fighting the English.'

Suddenly the sun went behind a cloud and it became quite dark. The mountains round the loch looked purple.

'It's going to rain,' said Callum.

Rory hoped there would not be a storm making big waves on the loch. They pushed out the boat, and Callum pulled strongly on the oars. All at once Rory felt his hair stand on end. They had reached the middle of the loch when Rory caught sight of something in the water. It was moving toward them. It seemed to have a dark head—and was it one hump or two?

'Callum,' he cried in a shaky voice. 'It's the monster!'

Callum looked round. Rory waited, trembling. Then Callum laughed.

'That's not a monster, Rory. That's a tree trunk. Look, you can see the branches!'

Rory looked again. Callum was right. It was a tree trunk. Rory felt rather silly, but he was glad that it wasn't a monster.

It was a long climb up to the little whitewashed cottage. Granny was standing at the door, waiting for Rory.

'Come away in,' she said as he came panting up the path.

It had been a happy day, but by supper-time Rory was tired. He sat in the kitchen at the scrubbed wooden table, drinking a cup of milk from Granny's cow, Morag. The clock on the wall was ticking quietly. Rory felt his eyes closing as he watched its pendulum swinging backward and forward.

'Bed-time,' said Granny, and in no time at all she was tucking him up in bed in the little room next to the kitchen. The window was open and Rory could smell the honeysuckle which grew on the cottage wall.

'Sing me the song about Dream Angus, Granny,' he begged.

Dream Angus was the sandman who came walking over the heather in the twilight, with his sack of dreams to sell to children. Granny sang in her soft, lilting voice:

'Birds are nestling, nestling together,
Dream Angus is coming over the
                         heather.
         Dreams to sell,
         Fine dreams to sell,
         Angus is here
         With dreams to sell.
Hush, my baby and sleep without
                         fear;
Dream Angus has brought you a
                         dream my dear.'

When Granny stopped singing Rory's eyes were closed. He was asleep. He was smiling. Dream Angus had brought him a fine dream.